Science Alive!
Earth and the Solar System

CRABTREE
Publishing Company
www.crabtreebooks.com

How to use this book

Each chapter begins with experiments, followed by the explanation of the scientific concepts used in the experiments. Each experiment is graded according to its difficulty level. A level 4 or 5 means adult assistance is advised. Difficult words are in boldface and explained in the glossary on page 32.

Crabtree Publishing
www.crabtreebooks.com

PMB 16A, 350 Fifth Avenue,
Suite 3308, New York
New York 10118

612 Welland Avenue,
St. Catharines, Ontario
Canada L2M 5V6

**Published in 2003
by Crabtree Publishing Company**

Published with Times Editions
Copyright © 2003 by Times Media Private Limited

Series originated and designed by
TIMES EDITIONS
An imprint of Times Media Private Limited
A member of the Times Publishing Group

Coordinating Editor: Ellen Rodger
Project Editor: Carrie Gleason
Production Coordinator: Rosie Gowsell
Series Writers: Darlene Lauw, Lim Cheng Puay
Series Editor: Oh Hwee Yen
Title Editor: Oh Hwee Yen
Series Designers: Rosie Francis, Geoslyn Lim
Series Picture Researcher: Susan Jane Manuel

Cataloging-in-Publication Data
Lauw, Darlene.
  Earth and the solar system / Darlene Lauw and Lim Cheng Puay.
    p. cm. — (Science alive!)
  Summary: Introduces concepts related to our solar system and Earth's
place in it through various activities and projects.
Includes bibliographical references and index.
  ISBN 0-7787-0569-2 (RHB : alk. paper) — ISBN 0-7787-0615-X (PB : alk. paper)
  1. Solar system—Juvenile literature. 2. Earth—Juvenile literature.
[1. Solar system. 2. Earth.] I. Lim, Cheng Puay. II. Title. III. Series.
  QB501.3 .L38 2002
  523.2—dc21

                                                    2002013742
                                                    LC

Picture Credits
Marc Crabtree: cover; AFP: 22 (bottom), 26 (bottom); Art Directors & Trip Photo Library: 6 (bottom), 7 (top), 10 (bottom),
14 (bottom), 15 (bottom), 30 (bottom), 31 (bottom); Getty Images/Hulton Archive: 18 (top), 27 (middle); Photobank
Photolibrary/Singapore: 1; Topham Picturepoint: 6 (top), 7 (middle), 11 (bottom), 15 (middle), 18 (bottom), 19 (middle),
23 (top and middle), 27 (top, right), 31 (top)

Printed and bound in Malaysia
1 2 3 4 5 6—0S—07 06 05 04 03 02

INTRODUCTION

There are nine planets in the solar system: Mercury, Venus, Earth, Mars, Jupiter, Saturn, Uranus, Neptune, and Pluto. Have you ever wondered what else makes up our solar system? Is the moon a planet? What is a comet? Why is Earth the only planet that supports life? Learn the secrets of Earth and the solar system through the experiments in this book.

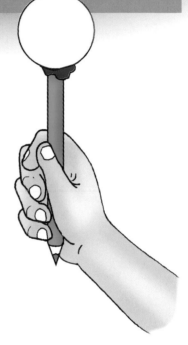

Contents

Around the sun

Hundreds of years ago, people believed the sun and all the planets in our solar system revolved around Earth. In reality, Earth and the other eight planets revolve around the sun. Try this activity to see how the planets orbit the sun.

You will need:
- A pocketknife
- Ten styrofoam balls of varying sizes, including two medium-sized balls of the same size
- Paints
- Paintbrushes
- A ruler
- A poster board
- A pencil
- String
- Glue

Model of the solar system

1 Using the pocketknife, slice each of the styrofoam balls in half. Ask an adult to help you.

2 Paint the balls according to the chart below. For example, your largest ball will be the sun, so paint it yellow.

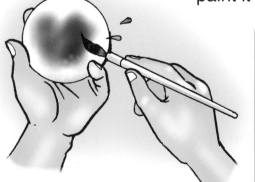

size	Planet	Color
largest ball	Sun	yellow
	Jupiter	dark yellow
	Saturn	brown
Uranus and Neptune are the same size!	Uranus	light turquoise
	Neptune	deep blue
	Earth	blue
	Venus	brown and orange
	Mars	red
	Mercury	dark gray
smallest ball	Pluto	light gray

3 Using the ruler and pencil, mark a dot 5 inches (13 cm) from the left edge of the board. Mark a second dot 5 inches (13 cm) from the first dot. Then mark eight dots, one every 2 to 3 inches (6 to 7.5 cm).

4 Tie a loop on one end of the string, place the pencil through the loop and stand the pencil's point on the second dot. Pull the string outward to stretch over the first dot. Hold the string and move the pencil across the poster board to draw the large part of a circle. Repeat for the other dots.

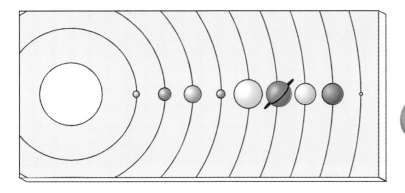

5 Glue the styrofoam planets onto the dots.

6 Label the planets. You have made a three-dimensional model of the solar system.

The color of sunshine

1 Fill the glass jar with cold water until the jar is almost full. Add the milk to the water, and stir with the spoon.

Difficult — 5
 — 4
Moderate — 3
 — 2
Easy — 1

You will need:
- A glass jar
- Cold water
- A teaspoon of milk
- A spoon
- A flashlight

2 Shine the flashlight through the side of the jar as shown in the diagram. What is the color of the water?

3 Now, hold the flashlight at the neck of the jar, facing you. What is the color of the water now?

The solar system

Our solar system contains the nine planets, the sun, and other **celestial bodies**. These include asteroids, which are small planets, meteors, which are solid **particles**, and comets, which are frozen balls of ice. In the experiment *Model of the Solar System*, you arranged the nine planets according to the way they appear in our solar system.

The nine planets revolve around the sun, each turning on its own **axis**. The number of hours one planet takes to make a complete turn on its axis is known as a day. Earth's day is 24 hours. Jupiter's day is ten hours long, the shortest of the planets in the solar system. A day on Venus, on the other hand, is 5,832 hours long! Jupiter has shorter days because it spins at a high speed on its axis, and Venus' day is longer because it spins at a lower speed.

A planet's orbit, or the number of days a planet takes to circle the sun, is known as a year. The farther the planet is from the sun, the longer its years are. A year on Earth is 365 days long. A year on Pluto, the planet farthest from the sun, is 248 Earth years long!

Nicolaus Copernicus

Ancient **astronomers** believed the sun and the rest of the planets revolved around Earth. In 1530, a **Roman Catholic** priest named Nicolaus Copernicus (1473–1543;

left) published a book that said Earth was not the center of the universe. Copernicus showed how Earth spins on an axis and orbits the sun along with the other planets. His ideas were met with anger by the Roman Catholic Church. The Church banned his book for 300 years but Copernicus' ideas changed the science of astronomy forever.

Did you know?
The sun is a star. The diameter of the sun is about 109 times that of Earth. In fact, the sun is so large it can fit 1.3 million Earths. The sun is the only star in our solar system, but there are many, many stars in the universe outside our solar system.

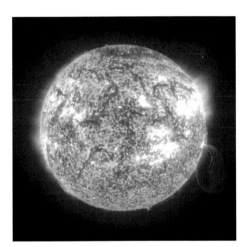

THE COLOR OF THE SUN

Sunlight is made up of all the colors you see in a rainbow. Some of these colors reflect off dust, **water vapor**, and other particles in air. The distance the light travels also affects the reflection of colors. More light is reflected when light travels a longer distance.

At dawn and dusk, the sun is low in the sky, and rays of sunlight travel a longer distance to reach Earth. Rays of violet, indigo, and blue are scattered, leaving rays of red and orange to color the sky. This is why the sky looks pink at these times of the day. At other times of the day, less violet, indigo, and blue light is scattered, and the sky looks blue.

Why does Earth move around the sun?

Why do the planets in the solar system move around the sun? What keeps the planets from crashing into each other, or from straying from their orbital paths? Try these experiments to understand orbital forces.

Difficult — 5
— 4
Moderate — 3
— 2
Easy — 1

You will need:
• A marble
• A jam jar with a lid

Spinning in circles

1 Place the marble in the jar as shown in the diagram.

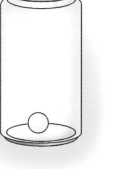

2 Close the lid and lay the jar on the ground. Move the jar in a circular motion. Continue doing this. Do you see the marble moving in circles, together with the jar?

3 Now, move the jar faster. While you are moving the jar, slowly turn the jar until it is in a vertical position. Stop moving the jar. What do you see?

Like the moon, artificial satellites, made by humans, revolve around Earth. These satellites help send telephone and television signals from one part of the globe to another. Scientists and **engineers** launch the satellites into space using rockets. How do they get the satellites to return to Earth?

You will need:
- A compass
- A pencil or pen
- A piece of stiff paper
- Scissors
- A ruler
- Tape
- A jar
- A marble

Back to Earth

 Use the compass to draw a circle with a diameter of about 24 inches (60 cm) on the stiff paper. Cut the circle out.

 Next, divide the circle into eight sectors as shown in the diagram. Cut out one sector.

 Tape the two cut edges of the remaining sectors together to form a cone.

 Now, fit the cone, pointing downward, into the jar. Secure the cone to the jar with tape.

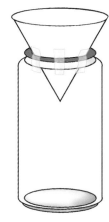

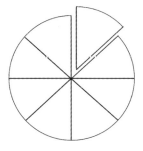 Put the marble into the cone. Move the jar in fast, small circles. Do you see the marble moving toward the top edge of the cone?

Make the marble slow down. What do you see?

9

Orbiting, orbiting...

In the experiment *Spinning in Circles*, the marble in the jar continued spinning even after you stopped moving the jar. Why does this happen? A force known as **centripetal force** was acting on the marble, which kept it moving in a circular motion. Earth and other planets revolve around the sun because of centripetal force. Imagine a string attaching the planets to the sun. This pulling force the string exerts on each planet is like its centripetal force. Without it, the planets will fly off in a straight line, away from the sun!

In the experiment *Back to Earth*, the marble moved to the upper edge of the cone if you moved it fast enough. When you slowed down, the marble fell into the cone, under the influence of Earth's gravity. **Gravitational force** is what pulls satellites toward Earth. Satellites keep their orbits by maintaining speed. When the speed of satellites drops beyond a certain point, they fall back to Earth.

Centripetal force acts on objects moving in a circular motion, such as these bicycles (*below*) making a turn.

QUIZTIME

The sun rises in the east and sets in the west. Can you use this information to guess the direction of Earth's spin?

Answer: Yes, Earth spins from west to east.

The first satellite

The former Soviet Union launched the first artificial satellite into orbit around Earth. It was called *Sputnik* (*above*), the Russian word for satellite. *Sputnik* orbited Earth for three months at a speed of about 17,360 miles per hour (27,932 km per hour). During its orbit, *Sputnik* gathered valuable information about the ionosphere, a layer of Earth's atmosphere, and temperatures in space.

COSPAS-SARSAT

The COSPAS-SARSAT satellite system was the result of an international effort by the United States, Canada, France, and the former Soviet Union. This system is used for ground and sea search-and-rescue missions and has saved thousands of lives. COSPAS-SARSAT comprises four satellites in orbit above Earth's North and South Poles. These satellites pick up distress signals and send the location of these signals to rescue teams around the world. When a distress call is received, the nearest rescue team rushes to the scene.

Did you know?
There are about 8,000 human-made objects orbiting Earth! Of these, 2,500 are satellites (*above*). The rest of the objects include debris such as the lenses of space cameras, rocket bodies, and hatch covers from spacecraft.

11

Our Earth is a giant spinning top!

Earth revolves around the sun once every 24 hours. Day and night happen because Earth rotates on an axis. You can see Earth's rotation with this experiment.

■ **Ask an adult for help**

Difficult — 5
— 4
Moderate — 3
— 2
Easy — 1

You will need:
- A stick
- A piece of string
- A rock

Shadowing the sun

1 Push the stick into the ground. Ask an adult to help you if you have trouble with this.

 2 Stretch the string along the shadow of the stick. Use the rock to hold the string in place as shown in the diagram. Can you work out where the string's shadow will be in three hours time?

If you live anywhere north of the equator, the sun is at the south at midday. Shadows that fall around this time are at their shortest. You can use the sun to help you find where you are.

You will need:
- A map of your neighborhood with "north," "south," "east," and "west" written on it
- An analog watch

Sun guide

1 On a clear, sunny day, pick a place you want to go to on the map. Place the watch on the map.

2 Turn the watch until its hour hand points at the sun.

3 The line between the number 12 on the watch's face and its hour hand points to the south. Remove the watch from the map, but hold it close to the map. Slowly turn the map such that its south is in alignment with the invisible dividing line on the watch's face. Use the watch as a compass to help you find your way.

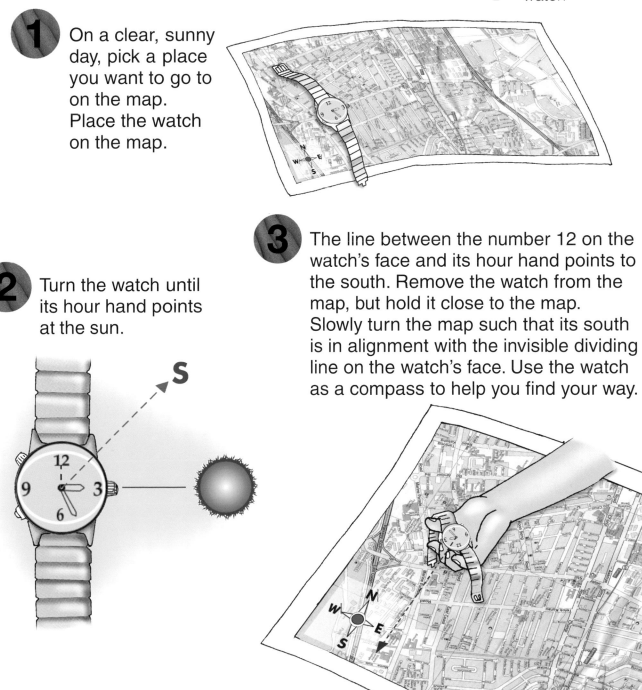

Earth, a giant spinning top

Earth behaves like a giant spinning top. It spins on its axis and makes one complete round every 24 hours. The sun appears to move around in a complete circle, but it is Earth that is actually moving. The stick in the experiment *Shadowing the Sun* was a simple sundial (*below*). A sundial is an instrument that tells the time of day by following the shadows of the sun. If you watched the stick's shadow all day, you would see that it makes one complete circle in 24 hours.

Why do the planets spin as they orbit the sun? Some scientists think that the spinning action started when the planets formed in the solar system 4.55 billion years ago. Before the planets formed, a thick cloud of gas spun around the sun. Over time, the gas condensed into particles, or small pieces, of dust. These specks of dust merged with other dust particles revolving around the sun. They became bigger and bigger until they grew to the size of the planets in the solar system! As more and more dust particles condensed and merged to form planets, they started to spin more vigorously. This is why planets spin!

Central vision

Many ancient astronomers in Greece developed theories to explain how Earth spun. It was originally thought that Earth was the center of the universe and that the stars in the night sky rotated around Earth. Greek astronomer Aristarchus (310–230 B.C.) of Samos had a theory that it was Earth that spun, and not the stars. The spinning of Earth explained why the pattern of the stars seemed to move from east to west.

Did you know?
All the planets in our solar system, with the exception of Earth, are named after Roman gods. For example, Mercury is named after the Roman messenger god with wings and Venus is the name of the Roman god of love. Mars is the Roman god of war, and Neptune (*below*) is the Roman god of the sea.

THE MOON'S FACE

The moon spins around Earth just like Earth spins around the sun. Earth takes a day, or 24 hours, to revolve once on its axis and the moon takes approximately 27 days. From Earth we always see the moon from the same side. This is because the moon also takes 27 days to circle Earth.

Orbit of the planets

All the known planets in our solar system orbit the sun. The planets are always moving around the sun in **ellipse**-shaped orbits. Try this activity to duplicate a planet's orbit.

Difficult — 5
— 4
Moderate — 3
— 2
Easy — 1

You will need:
- A ruler
- A piece of cardboard
- A pencil
- Pencil crayons
- Sticky tack
- A piece of string

Foci fun

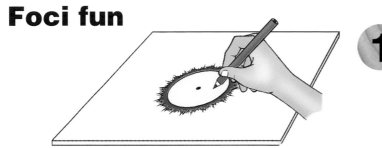

1 Put a dot at the exact center of the cardboard. Draw and color a sun around the dot.

2 Make a second pencil dot 2 inches (5 cm) from the first dot.

3 Attach a piece of sticky tack to each dot. Tie the string together and stick two sides to the sticky tack.

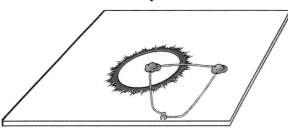

4 Place the pencil against the inside of the string and move the pencil around in a circular manner until it is back at the starting point. You have just drawn an ellipse, or the shape of a planet's orbit.

The sun provides Earth with both daylight and warmth, but what about the other planets? How hot is it on Venus and how cold on Jupiter? This simple experiment explains how a planet's distance from the sun affects its temperature.

Difficult – 5
– 4
Moderate – 3
– 2
Easy – 1

You will need:
- A 60-watt light bulb screwed into a socket such as a lamp
- A piece of white paper
- A ruler
- A pen

Hot stuff

 1 Turn the light on a minute before you begin your observation.

2 On the piece of paper, use the ruler to measure distances from the bulb's surface, such as 1/2 inch (1.3 cm), 1 inch (2.5 cm), 1 1/2 inches (3.8 cm), up to 4 1/2 inches (11.4 cm).

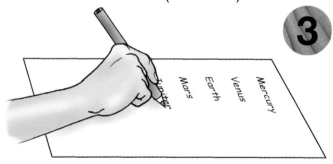

3 Write the planets in order according to their distance from the sun: Mercury, Venus, Earth, Mars, Jupiter, Saturn, Uranus, Neptune, and Pluto.

 4 Place your hand at the intervals and record your observations about how hot your hand feels and how much light the bulb gives off at each interval.

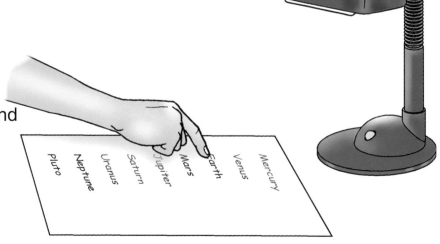

17

Centered around the sun

The word "planet" means wanderer in ancient Greek. The Greeks observed that the planets seemed to travel throughout the year. This traveling, later called an orbit, is elliptical in shape and has the sun as its center. In the *Foci Fun* experiment, you recreated the oval-shaped orbit of a planet, called an ellipse. A circle has one center point, but an ellipse has two foci. In a planet's orbit, the sun is one focus and dark space is the other.

The sun's heat and light, in the form of solar energy, is greater on the planets closer to the sun. In the *Hot Stuff* experiment, your observations showed that the planets closest to the sun, Mercury and Venus, were hotter than the rest of the planets.

Copernicus had the right idea when he drew this diagram of our solar system (*above*) showing the planets revolving around the sun.

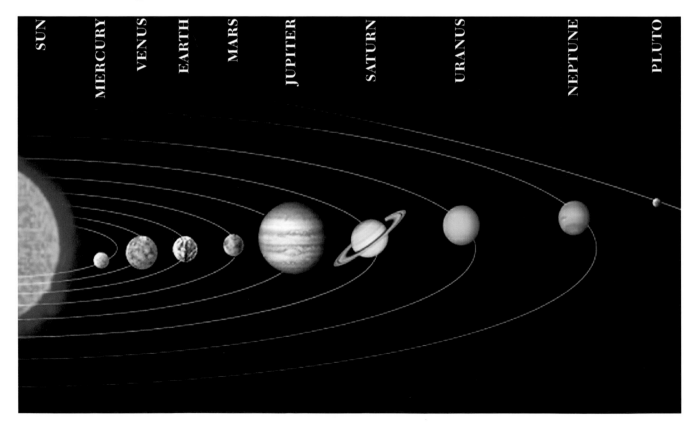

SUN MERCURY VENUS EARTH MARS JUPITER SATURN URANUS NEPTUNE PLUTO

Planetary motion

Johannes Kepler (1571–1630; *below*) was a German mathematician and astronomer who took the ideas of Copernicus and developed them further. Kepler developed three laws of planetary motion:

1) Planets orbit the sun in ellipses.
2) Planets move faster when they are closer to the sun.
3) The length of a planet's year depends on the planet's distance from the sun.

Scientist Sir Isaac Newton (1642–1727) said that every object in the universe had its own gravity. The sun, Earth, moon, and planets all have gravity. The sun's gravity keeps the planets aligned and in orbit. Newton developed a theory of gravity after watching an apple fall from a tree in an orchard. He thought that if Earth's force of gravity made the apple fall downward, then the same force would apply in space.

QUIZTIME

You need to travel several light years from one planet to another. Are light years a measure of time?

Answer: No! In fact, light years are used to measure distances. One light year is 5.88 trillion miles (9.46 trillion km).

Did you know
The planet Uranus is so far from the sun that temperatures are a frosty -345°F (-210°C).

A LONG DAY ON MERCURY

Mercury is the closest planet to the sun and the second smallest planet in the solar system. A year on Mercury is just 88 days, but a day on Mercury is longer than its year, because it rotates on its axis much slower than it rotates on its orbit. Mercury is an incredibly hot 840°F (450°C) during its day and -275°F (-170°C) at night. Nothing lives on Mercury because the planet has no real atmosphere.

What is out there?

Have you ever seen a falling star or observed a comet through a telescope? Asteroids, meteors, and comets have amazed and baffled people for centuries. Try these experiments to understand why.

You will need:
- A digital thermometer
- A pencil or pen
- A notebook

Fast and hot

 Put the thermometer in your hands and hold it for thirty seconds. In the notebook, record the temperature on the thermometer.

2 Put the thermometer aside and vigorously rub your hands together for fifteen seconds.

 Pick the thermometer up and hold it for another thirty seconds. Record the temperature.

Try this experiment to find out the shape of an asteroid.

Asteroid light

You will need:
- A sheet of paper
- Tape
- A pencil
- A wall painted a light color
- A flashlight

1 Crumple the paper into a loose ball.

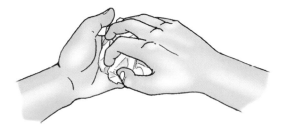

2 Tape the ball of paper to the pencil.

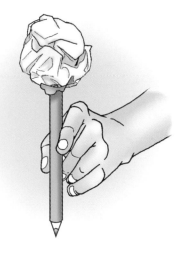

3 Using the wall as a screen, turn the lights out in the room and hold the flashlight in one hand to the side of the wall, with its bulb pointing away from the wall. The wall screen and the flashlight should be at an angle of 45 degrees.

4 Put the paper ball in front of the flashlight so that light reflects off the ball and onto the wall. Adjust the angle of the flashlight and rotate the pencil while observing the light reflected on the wall.

Faster than a speeding meteor

Asteroids, meteors (*below*), and comets are space travelers of a different sort. Asteroids are hunks of rock or metal that orbit the sun, mostly in a zone between the orbits of Mars and Jupiter called the asteroid belt. Comets are balls of ice, gas, and rocky dirt that circle the sun in a long, oval orbit. Meteors are pieces of asteroids that have fallen to Earth. In the *Fast and Hot* experiment, you discovered how **friction** makes a meteor hot. When it passes through Earth's atmosphere, the meteor is moving so fast that much or all of it burns up. The friction of your hands rubbing together produces heat as well. The temperature rose several degrees after you rubbed your hands together.

In the second experiment, *Asteroid Light*, you saw how the light reflected by the paper ball changed as the ball was rotated. Like the paper ball, asteroids are irregularly shaped lumps that rotate in space. The flashlight represented the sun. The brightness of the light reflecting off the ball changed continuously. Scientists study the different amounts of light reflected by an asteroid to determine its shape.

Edmund Halley

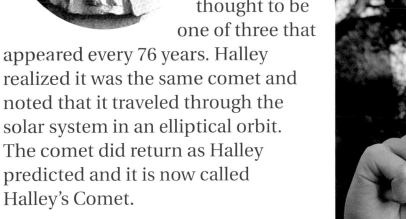

Edmund Halley (1656–1743; *left*) was a scientist who made many important discoveries. Using historical records, Halley accurately predicted a comet's return to Earth. The comet was originally thought to be one of three that appeared every 76 years. Halley realized it was the same comet and noted that it traveled through the solar system in an elliptical orbit. The comet did return as Halley predicted and it is now called Halley's Comet.

This boy on the right holds a piece of a meteorite that fell to Earth.

QUIZTIME

What is the difference between a meteor and a meteorite?

Answer: A meteor is a piece of space debris that burns up as it enters Earth's atmosphere. A meteorite is a meteor that has fallen to Earth.

KILLED BY A FALLING STAR

Some scientists think that the death of dinosaurs was caused by an asteroid or comet crashing on Earth 65 million years ago. The asteroid or comet landed in the Caribbean Sea, releasing large amounts of **flammable** gas from the ocean into the atmosphere. Fires broke out, covering the planet with smoke, dust, and soot so thick no sunlight could shine through. Earth became freezing cold and no plants could grow. As a result, the dinosaurs died of cold and hunger.

Did you know?
Astronomers believe comets "last" several hundred thousand years in our solar system. The warmth of the sun heats the frozen ice and gases in the comets, turning them into steam and glowing gases. Eventually, the comets "die."

Stargazing

When you look at the moon in the night sky, you see a different picture every night. Sometimes you cannot see the moon at all. Find out why this happens by doing this experiment.

You will need:
- A small rubber ball
- A pencil
- Silly Putty™ or modeling clay
- A darkened room
- A flashlight
- A pencil or pen
- A notebook

Moonphase

1 Stick the ball securely to the end of the pencil using the putty or modeling clay.

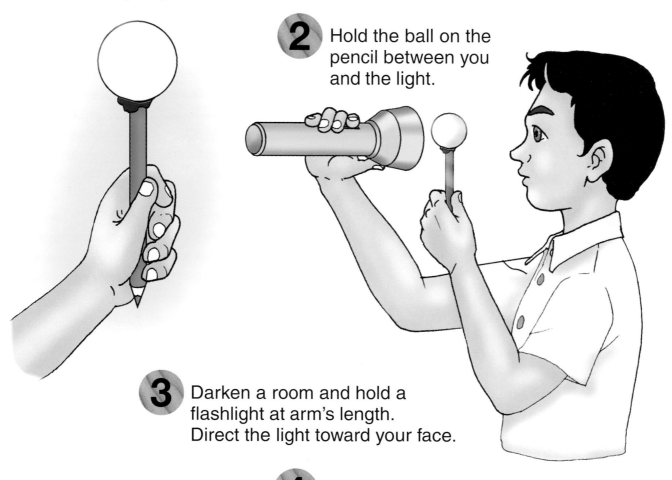

2 Hold the ball on the pencil between you and the light.

3 Darken a room and hold a flashlight at arm's length. Direct the light toward your face.

4 Record your observations. Is the ball easy to see?

Light and distance also affects a star's brightness. This experiment shows how.

Starbright

Difficult — 5
— 4
Moderate — 3
— 2
Easy — 1

You will need:
- A wall in a darkened room
- A flashlight
- A pencil or pen
- A notebook

1 Stand in the darkened room and shine a flashlight at the wall.

2 Walk toward the wall and observe the light pattern that is produced on the wall.

3 Walk away from the wall and observe the light pattern. Record your observations.

Sunlight, moonlight, and starlight

The moon appears bright in the night sky on certain days of the month. This "moonshine" happens because the moon reflects light from the sun. The side of the moon that faces the sun is always sunlit and the side that faces away from the sun is always dark. In the *Moonphase* experiment, you simulated a phase of the moon where the moon's surface was illuminated by the sun. Moonlight is a reflection of the sun's light. The moon's phases occur as it travels around Earth in orbit, when different parts of the moon's bright side are seen.

In the *Starbright* experiment, you found that the closer you were to the wall, the brighter and smaller, or more concentrated, the light was. Stars are giant sources of light. Stars that are closer to Earth appear brighter and more concentrated. A star farther away from Earth has **diffused light**. The sun and other stars are **luminous**, meaning they give off light. The moon and planets are not luminous and they reflect or bounce back light from the sun to Earth. Without the sun, the moon would not shine.

Using the sky

Before the 1400s, sailors in the Pacific Ocean and Indian Ocean used the position of the sun, planets, and the stars to help them find their way. By studying the position of the noonday sun, sailors could gauge how far north or south they were from the equator. The position of the north star helped sailors north of the equator estimate how far east or west they were to any place. Sailors south of the equator used the **southern cross** to direct them. From their observations, sailors drew star charts, maps, and designed compasses.

Early astronomers studied celestial bodies through telescopes such as the one on the left.

Do the other planets in our solar system have moons?

Answer: Yes, most of them do! Mars has two moons, called Deimos and Phobos. Jupiter has 28 known moons. One of them, Io, is shown below. Saturn has 30 known moons; Uranus has two known moons; Neptune has eight known moons and Pluto has one known moon called Charon. Space scientists are still discovering the moons of some planets.

Did you know?
Other stars in our galaxy are much brighter than our sun. The nearest star to the solar system, Alpha Centauri, is 58 trillion miles (97 trillion km) away from Earth.

A total eclipse of the moon (*left*) happens when the moon travels behind Earth so that Earth is between the moon and the sun. Earth blocks the light the moon receives from the sun and the moon is hidden in Earth's shadow.

MOON IN THE SKY

The phases of the moon are called the new moon, first quarter, full moon, and third quarter. We cannot see a new moon. The first quarter is seen as the right half and we see the full moon as the entire face of the moon. The third quarter is the left half of the moon. Use a calendar to see when these phases occur during the month and check them out for yourself.

27

Is there life out there?

Scientists say that the environment on most of the planets in our solar system cannot support life. The other planets are either too hot, too cold, or do not have water and the other conditions necessary to support life. Try this experiment to see how important a planet's surface temperature is.

You will need:
- Two large cookie jars or jam jars with lids
- Two thermometers, each small enough to fit into a jar

Too hot to live in

1 On a hot, sunny day, bring the jars and thermometers outside.

2 Place one of the thermometers into one of the jars and cover it with the lid.

3 Prop the other thermometer outside the other jar.

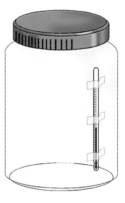

4 Leave the jars for an hour, then note the temperature on both thermometers.

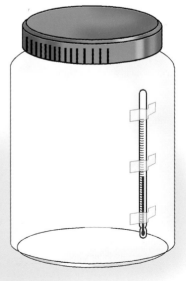

 WATCH OUT!
This experiment may not be possible with a digital thermometer. Digital thermometers are not designed to be left in humid conditions, such as in the jar, for more than fifteen minutes.

Why should we apply sunscreen when we go outdoors into the hot sun? Find out with this experiment!

Sunshield

 1 On a bright sunny day, lay the newspaper on a flat surface in the sun. Make sure that you set up your experiment in a place without any traffic. Tape the newspaper onto the surface.

Difficult — 5
        — 4
Moderate — 3
        — 2
Easy — 1

You will need:
- A sheet of newspaper
- Tape
- Sunscreen with a rating of at least SPF 30
- A sheet of transparency
- Four erasers

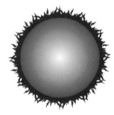 **2** Apply a thick layer of sunscreen onto the transparency. Position the erasers on the newspaper. Place the transparency on the erasers so that the transparency sits above the newspaper.

 3 Leave the transparency alone for a day. What do you see the next day?

The greenhouse effect and the ozone layer

At the end of the experiment *Too Hot to Live In*, the temperature inside the jar was much higher. This is because the glass of the jar trapped heat inside the jar and prevented it from escaping. The temperature inside the jar increased as a result. This is known as the greenhouse effect. Gases on a planet can also trap heat. The greenhouse effect is stronger on some planets and weaker on other planets in our solar system. On Venus, the greenhouse effect is so strong that the temperature on the surface reaches 900°F (482°C)!

Ozone is a pale blue, highly poisonous gas with a strong odor. Ozone is part of Earth's atmosphere. A layer of ozone lies between nine to 25 miles (15 to 40 km) above Earth's surface. This layer of ozone protects us from the full force of harmful **ultraviolet radiation** coming from the sun. In the *Sunshield* experiment, the sunscreen behaved like Earth's ozone layer. The portion of newspaper under the transparency remained white while the rest of the newspaper turned yellow. This happened because light from the sun reacted with the chemicals in the newspaper and turned it yellow. The portion of newspaper under the sunscreen was shielded from sunlight and so remained white.

Another Earth?

Mars (*below*) is the nearest planet to Earth. Like Earth, Mars has polar ice caps and a 24-hour day. Despite those similarities, things that live on Earth cannot live on Mars. There is not enough oxygen and water on Mars to support life. Temperatures on the surface of Mars are extreme, ranging from just below freezing point to above boiling temperatures. These conditions are too harsh to support life.

Scientists think life may have existed on Mars four billion years ago. Researchers have found evidence of dried-up lakes, rivers, and even oceans more than 328 feet (100 m) deep. The temperature on Mars was also probably not as extreme as it is now.

June 26, 2001

The glass windows of a greenhouse (*left*) stops the sun's heat from leaving the greenhouse. Plants use this heat to grow during the winter and in cold climates. Clouds behave like the glass windows of a greenhouse, trapping heat within the atmosphere of Earth, and keeping us warm.

CHLOROFLUOROCARBONS

Certain chemicals known as chlorofluorocarbons (CFCs) damage the ozone layer. Hair sprays (*right*) and refrigerator **coolant** often contain CFCs. When these chemicals are released, they rise to the ozone layer and break ozone **molecules** down. This is why governments around the world now ban the use of CFCs.

Glossary

astronomy (page 7): The science that studies Earth, the solar system, space objects, and galaxies.

axis (page 6): A straight line on which an object turns. Earth's axis passes through the North and South Poles.

celestial body (page 6): Something relating to the sky or space. Planets and comets are celestial bodies.

centripetal force (page 10): A force moving or directed toward a center or axis.

coolant (page 31): A substance that draws off heat and produces cooling.

diffused light (page 26): Light that is less bright because it is spread out.

ellipse (page 16): An egg-shaped circle.

engineers (page 9): People who work in a branch of engineering. Engineering is the science of designing and building structures, products, and systems such as railroads and hydroelectric plants.

flammable (page 23): Able to catch fire easily.

friction (page 22): The resistance objects face when rubbing against each other.

gravitational force (page 10): The force of gravity, or the attraction on objects to the surfaces of planets.

luminous (page 26): Something that gives off light.

molecules (page 31): The smallest particles of matter, consisting of one or more atoms.

particle (page 6): A very small amount or piece of something.

Roman Catholic (page 7): A member of the Christian Church governed by the Pope, who is its head, in Rome.

satellite (page 7): An object that orbits another in space. Some satellites are made on Earth and launched into space to perform functions such as communications.

southern cross (page 27): A constellation of four stars shaped like a cross in the southern hemisphere.

ultraviolet radiation (page 30): Invisible energy waves.

water vapor (page 7): A fine mist or gas formed from heating a solid or liquid.

Index